THE CONSERVATIVE AND LIBERAL POLITICAL LEADERS IN NIGERIA POLITICS

A VIEW OF NIGERIAN POLITICAL SYSTEM AND THE ANCIENT POLITICAL SYSTEM BEFORE AND AFTER THE DEATH OF JESUS CHRIST

OMON PERIS EGBON

Nigeria as we all know is multi-facet system in which various political office holders seek for with almost priority to win election whether do or die process.

The Nigeria system has gone down the drain where all can see the recent development of election which is being intimated by one political system and wants' to gain territorial control to subdue others for them to explore all necessary power and vote.

The recent trend in politics is no longer new to us though we thought that the previous administration of President Goodluck Jonathan maintain a good and free play zone for all political party that gave us hope and posterity to all Nigerians thinking Nigeria Electoral process has come to stay and expected the current government to maintain the status quo but the reverse is the case. We have come to see that all that the former government did has been chartered to the drain and washed into the pit of hell by a number of deceitful people.

The bible says when a bad ruler rules a nation, that nation is bound to be a failure, goes into recession, and crumbled into the pit of poverty. It took President Jonathan just few weeks to conduct free and fair election and we all see the wonders and written hands of God upon him, but the day, the new political office holder of the current government came into office and up till now election has become a shambo, thrown to the pit, and a failure in Nigeria and the rest of Africa who depended on Nigeria as an example to follow.

I write not to shame anyone but to correct the mistake and failure of our past and current leaders who fight for selfish interest and concerned about their own personal pocket and Nigerians at large mostly the youth who sell their right to earn a pot of pottage and forgetting about their future. Because of this, I sat down and try to illustrate the Nigerian Political System and the Political System before and after the death of Jesus Christ.

I called this **The Liberal and Conservative Leaders (known as the Pharisees and Sadducees)**and till today, it still existsbetween us and Nigeria as large.

First of all, who are Pharisees and Sadducees and who are the Liberal and Conservative Leaders. Let's draw a line here;

Pharisees as seen in the bible are the minority members in the society and were middle class businessmen.

The Pharisees related well and had direct contact with the common men in Israel and were held of high esteem more than the Sadducees.

They gave oral tradition and equal authority to the written word of God.

The Pharisees accepted the written word of God as inspired by God.

They obeyed the tradition of God's word as given by Moses in the Old Testament

(Deuteronomy 4:2). However, the Pharisees did remain true to Gods word.

The Pharisees never allow their relationship to be equal with God or to be reduced to legalistic lists of rules and rituals.

The Pharisees believe in the following;

> i. Believe in the resurrection of the dead (Act 23:6).
>
> ii. Believe in after life with an appropriate punishment and reward on an individual basis.
>
> iii.   They believe God control all things, yet decision made by a person also contributed to the course of one's life.
>
> iv.   They believe Angels and demons exist (Act 23:8).

The Sadducees on the other hand were the major leaders in Israel then before the fall of Jerusalem by Rome and held 70% of all seats in the government chambers. They were called as the ruling council named **SANNEDRIN** and worked alongside with the decision of Rome.

The Sadducees relied on the decisions made by the Pharisees because they were closer to the common men of the society than them (Sadducees).

The Sadducees were the wealthy class and never associated well with the common people except the Pharisees.

They Sadducees were responsible for the death of Jesus and James the Apostle and they were more into politics than religion and were never common with Jesus Christ.

The Sadducees considered only the written word to be from God and preserved the word of God especially the book of Moses (Genesis through Deuteronomy) and were never perfect in their doctrinal views.

The Sadducees held a belief contrary to the scripture, which are as follows;

i. They were extremely self-sufficient to the point of denying God's involvement in everyday life.

ii. They deny any resurrection of the dead. (Matthew 22:23, Mark 12:18-27, Acts 23:8).

iii. They deny any after life, holding that soul perished at death and therefore denying penalty or reward after the earthly life.

iv.   They deny the existence of a spiritual world (i.e. Angels and demons, Act 23:8).

Now let's point out here who are the Liberals and Conservative Leaders.

The Liberals are the Pharisees who neverreduced their standard to be equal with God but accepted all doctrines given to Moses by God and believe in spirituality and life after death including the existence of demons and Angels.

While the Sadducees are the conservative leaders who don't give concern about God and his laws and conduct including not believing in after life and spirituality. They never believe that Christ Jesus resurrected from the dead and existence of demons and Angels.

Let's picture this scenario to the Nigerian Political System.

The All Progressive Congress (APC) is what I call the conservative leaders who consist of Pharisees and Sadducees. They control all the affairs of government and do whatever pleases them and don't care about the concerns of the masses i.e. the common men. Though talk of change but yet are the most corrupt leaders and holds down the wealth of the nation.

The People's Democratic Party are the liberal leaders though still consist of Pharisees and Sadducees. They have little concerns for the masses i.e. the common men and make sure there is distribution of wealth across the nation though they are still corrupt and believe in God unlike the APC.

We have seen this today in Nigeria were the APC the Sadducees have not been able to equally meet up with the demand of the masses i.e. the common men in Nigeria and left the nation grounded and broke without no concern for what will happen the economy growth and wealth maximization. They squander all resources saying they are fighting corruption and bring up unnecessary news about certificate, health issues, and unwanted stories that will keep the nation plunge under chaos and confusion not doing what they were sent to do.

I was watching the news one day and saw that the law to stop the use of traditional mark pass through first reading the scale through second reading and begin to wonder if these political office holdersare children or fools? Laws that are better to legislate on is thrown away and dumped into the trash can because they enslave Nigerians so that they can come and beg them for food whenever it's time to contest again for election.

Remember that Jesus always had issues with the Sadducees but a little with the Pharisees because they always try to find fault in anything he did or say and the Sadducees ganged up with the Pharisees to put him to death because they were afraid he will bring unwanted Roman attention . This can easily be seen in her political system in Nigeria today where the Christian join hands alongside with the Pegans (Unbelievers)and Muslim to destroy the church, kill the political system all because of personal gain and greediness forgetting that the bible says *for the government shall be upon the shoulders of the Christians and the church itselfwhich is the manifold wisdom of God upon the body of Christ as a representative of him upon the earth*and were supposed to be taking orders and advice from the body of Christ but the reverse is the case today where law makers who are Christian who is expected to protect the body of Christ pass laws that will abolished the church system and how they are expected to worship their God and break down the entity of God.

We have seen today, that even the so-called Christian Politicians who are in various political office conspired with Muslim and devilish society to put to death innocent souls all because of personal gain and wealth accumulation. They don't mind who they clear out of the way just to get to the pick of their political height and fulfilment. They murder fellow believers and not even afraid of the consequences that follows next; they are now too familiar with most Pastors and so called men of God who even join them in perpetrating this bastard act forgetting that evil will never go unpunished.

The current trend in Nigeria has make me wonder if truly we have believers who really stand for God and put down laws that seems not to favour we as Christians. Most Christians who acquire this political office don't give a dem or concern whether the church should move forward or not. The Muslim can use all they have to build Mosque and sponsor terrorism against we Christians and the Politicians who call themselves Christians fold their hands and watch things go bad and destroyed. Should we now call this one's Christians or persecutors of the body of Christ? I cannot separate them from those killers and Muslims who make sure they engrave and enslave Christians to their death.

We have seen in the Northern Part of Nigeria today how fellow Christians are killed because they not Muslim and refuses to join the Muslim race which they call

Islamism. Thousands of souls have been murdered in cold blood without the federal government even saying anything in regards to it because they are all Muslim agenda to suffocate the Christian until we bow to them which is not possible. If you are current with news, you will discover that the day a Fulani herdsman is killed; numerous force menwill be discharge to bring to justice the perpetrators while if the Fulani herdsmen kill a Christian nothing is said concerning it; this is a good example of Southern Kaduna and Ife in Osun State.

Let's take a good look at the recent concluded presidential election in U.S were we saw the outcome of Donald Trump victory over Hillary Clinton. Who among them can one consider as a Pharisees

(Liberals) and Sadducees (Conservative)? Donald Trump is not really a strong Christian but believe God exist while Hillary Clinton is just there as one who is standing on the fence. Then tell me, why will Donald Trump not win the election? It was a miracle and it was never depended on people's vote but God who made it possible and happened that way for his purpose on earth so that Christianity will not be doomed or affected by Islamism or illuminati agenda. Immediately Donald Trump became President, we saw different measures put in place to sustain the gospel and aborted several laws laid down by former Presidency, Barrack Obama and previous administration just for the purpose of Christ. It simply tells there is still hope for us believers. He even advertised the conference program between Pastor Chris Oyakhilome and Benny Himmand said are you ready for this program? That's a man after God's purpose.

The Nigerian Political system has become worst more than before leaving no hope for the masses including the rich themselves. This is to tell you that government has nothing to offer to us as Nigerians for those who depend on them for survival. If truly the government is a government for the people, by the people and of the people, then, they should have been able to meet up with the demands of Nigerians and stop the killing of Christians and the allegation put before Apostle Johnson Suleman.

I watched a video where Apostle Johnson Suleman and Bishop David Oyedepo condemned the attack on Christians and told members to kill any Fulani herdsmen found around his church, I was really happy because who say a Christian cannot defend themselves? If we Christian who have big congregation don't speak out, how will the members of the church react or other Christians in the North feel when no High profile Pastors aren't saying anything.

After the comment by Apostle Johnson Suleman criticised the killings in Kaduna, the DSS and SSS try to arrest him in Ekiti but God saved by bringing the governor, Fayose to his rescue him. But what he the government don't know is that how which he was arrested Nigeria will not have been in peace. After this attack, came the Kaduna State governor, El Rufai who fall among the Sadducees (conservative) brought allegation against the man of God for no just reasoning because he was protecting his own fellow believers. That's to tell you that this people (Sadducees) are all out to wipe out Christians from Nigeria or force them to bow to them and thereby bringing Islamism to its fullest into Nigeria.

Every believer should seat up right and be a watch man because Islamism is growing at a great pace that is why we are seeing the killings today happening in our very before. They know that Christians cannot do anything physical to them but we say it's a lie from the pit of hell; we have a

God who can at once wipe those killers and there sponsors from this planet earth and no story will be left of them again. Our God is a merciful God and he never advised us to carry weapon as a means of defends on like the Muslims who their doctrine says kill them who refused to accept their beliefs.

Note here that, not because PDP is better off than APC, but the agenda of the current government and its APC members give us no doubt that they are all after personal gain, self-centred minded people who don't care if Nigeria survive or not. They bring several issues just to distract Nigerians, matter that do not concern us; such of which is the certificate of and the saga going on in the National Assembly between Custom Boss and Senators on the issue of Task fee which we later discover was because the Senate Leader did not register his Range Rover car according to the laws governing the Custom Service. Now ask me what is going to do to Nigerians? Will it provide a square meal for them? Definitely No.

I hereby advice the government to wake up from their slumber and be up doing, protect every Nigerians for no one is dog that is killed without no concern.

Whether you be a Sadducees or Pharisees, all government officials is duty bound to meet up with their responsibility as a leader appointed into office whether it be through election fraud or elected into office properly. For no office occupied by you is your fathers throne; for God made some so why others force themselves there. So act as leader and be responsible in your dealings.

Nigerians are one, so let no man or government think he is strongman to hold it down. We have seen great and powerful leaders in the world dethroned from their office and yours cannot be exempted. Take a case of former Head of State, Mohammed Abacha.

Let's all political office holders be at alert especially those in South-South, South East, South West, a sunami we see is coming and until you wake up and protect your chores and territory, they will sweep into it and wipe your people.

Long live Nigeria.

ABOUT AUTHOR

Omon Peris Egbon is young and vibrant individual whose purpose is to correct the indiscipline among youth and the society in general. He is geared towards correcting abnormalities in business, organization and the society at large. He is a graduate of Business Management from Federal Polytechnic, Auchi, Edo State, Nigeria.

He is a leader, writer, trainer, businessman who have been involved in helping others find out the great treasure hidden in them. He is the third of his parents and a junior twin.

He is part of a movement of youth that help to raise feeble men to become mighty men of valour called Kingdom Ambassador's Network Intl. He is skilled in putting various intellects together. He is social media manager, business & project manager, consultant, adviser to upcoming businesses and a Kingdom Addict and a member of Believers Loveworld Inc & Wisdom Christian Centre.

COMMENT

For more information and comment, please get back to me on mail.

egbonomon@gmail.com

+2347036529760, +23470457410259